Communities & Consequences

The Unbalancing of New Hampshire's Human Ecology,
and What We Can Do About It

Communities & Consequences

The Unbalancing of New Hampshire's Human Ecology,
and What We Can Do About It

Peter Francese
and
Lorraine Stuart Merrill

Peter E. Randall Publisher LLC
Portsmouth, New Hampshire 03802
2008

ISBN10: 1-931807-67-1
ISBN13: 978-1-931807-67-8

Library of Congress Control Number: 2007942819

Additional copies available from:
    Enfield Publishing & Distribution Company
    P.O. Box 699, Enfield, NH 03748
    Book orders: 888-216-7611
    Voice: 603-632-7377 • Fax: 603-632-5611
    email: info@enfieldbooks.com
    www.enfieldbooks.com

Peter E. Randall Publisher LLC
Box 4726, Portsmouth NH 03802
www.perpublisher.com

Book design: Grace Peirce

Book Web site: www.communitiesandconsequences.org

Photo credits: Unless otherwise noted, all photographs are from the documentary
Communities & Consequences *produced by Jay Childs, JBC Communications,*
www.jbc.com

Cover Photo: Residents at Hopkinton high school for 2007 annual town meeting.
Photo by Preston Gannaway, Concord Monitor.

Contents

Acknowledgments

We are extremely grateful to the many organizations and individuals here in New Hampshire that have provided both financial and editorial support for our work.

The following organizations are prime sponsors of this work:

Donahue, Tucker & Ciandella, PLLC
New Hampshire Association of Realtors
New Hampshire Business & Industry Association
New Hampshire Charitable Foundation
New Hampshire College & University Council
New Hampshire Hospital Association
New Hampshire Housing Finance Authority
Northeast Delta Dental
Public Service of New Hampshire
RiverWoods at Exeter
University System of New Hampshire

In addition we thank the following individuals for their support and work on behalf of this book: Charles Vadakin, Kevin Peterson, Callie Carr, Dan Smith, William Ray, Jim Bolduc and Tom Duffy.

We also deeply appreciate the generosity of so many individuals across New Hampshire who agreed to be interviewed for this book. They provided the human face behind the dry demographic facts about our state.

The authors are grateful to their spouses, John Merrill and Paula Francese, for review of the manuscript and for their patience as we worked on this book over the past year. But we have a special debt of gratitude to Paula Francese for her creation of the index and meticulous copy-editing work as advised by Doris Troy, the copy editor.

This book was originally conceived as a companion to the documentary film *Communities and Consequences,* produced by Jay Childs and associate producer Justin Francese. We appreciate their manuscript review as well as substantial assistance with providing illustrations and organizing the content.

Dedication

This book is dedicated to the many volunteers and others in the eight regional workforce housing coalitions in New Hampshire. We applaud their tireless efforts on behalf of workers across the state who simply need an affordable place to live. If any reader wishes to become involved with their local housing coalition the contact information is below.

Greater Concord Region
Contact: Rosemary Heard
CATCH Neighborhood Housing
Phone: (603) 225-8835
Email: rheard@catchhousing.org
Web: www.catchhousing.org

Monadnock Region
Contact: Susy Thielen
Heading for Home
Phone: (603) 352-1449
Email: SusyT@headingforhome.org
Web: www.headingforhome.org

Greater Manchester Region
Contact: Mike Skelton
Greater Manchester Chamber of
Commerce
Phone: (603) 666-6600 x107
Email: michaels@manchester-chamber.org
Web: www.manchester-chamber.org

Hanover/Lebanon Region
Contact: Anne Duncan Cooley
Upper Valley Housing Coalition
Phone: (802) 291-9100 x109
Email: adc@uvhc.org
Web: www.uvhc.org

Eastern Lakes Region
Contact: Edie DesMarais
Phone: (603) 569-2512
Email: desmarpe@metrocast.net

Seacoast Region
Contact: Diane Hartley
Workforce Housing Coalition
of the Greater Seacoast
Phone: (603) 431-3620
Email: info@seacoastwhc.org
Web: www.seacoastwhc.org

Greater Nashua Region
Contact: Lara Rice
Greater Nashua Workforce
Housing Coalition
Phone: (603) 459-0086
Email: lrice@gnwhc.org
Web: www.gnwhc.org

Mount Washington Region
Contact: Ed Butler
Mount Washington Valley
Housing Coalition
Phone: (603) 374-3940
Email: edofthenotch@aol.com

Introduction

THE IMPORTANCE OF BALANCE

Aerial view of Great Bay Estuarine system with farmland along the Squamscott River. photo by Sarah Thorne

The importance of balance and interrelationships in the natural environment is well understood. We know that a sharp decline of one species within an ecosystem can have serious, long-lasting negative consequences for all other life in the system. Each species plays an essential, although perhaps unseen or under-appreciated, role in the survival of the whole.

This same principle of ecological balance applies to the complexity of a human society. Loss or absence of members of one or another segment of a human community can have a profound impact on the health and prosperity of the whole. In New England, and particularly in our state of New Hampshire, we are starting to see that well-intentioned actions by members of small communities can have unfortunate long-term consequences for the region's inhabitants.

This book, along with its companion documentary and Web site, is our effort to show how a relatively small segment of the human ecosystem—the state of New Hampshire—is being substantially altered in just this way, to its economic and social detriment. The most significant and potentially most harmful consequence is the high out-migration of young adults. This exodus will leave New Hampshire with slowing workforce growth, declining numbers of children—the future workforce—and a population aging at an even faster rate due to increasing numbers of older residents.

This demographic shift appears to some as a natural change because of the aging baby boom generation. But most of it results from land-use and development choices made in the state's many, mostly small, communities—largely in reaction to increasing property taxes.

Towns and cities have made land-use decisions over the past decade in the context of a regional culture that values preservation over growth. That regional culture includes a strong attachment to the uniquely town-centered New England tradition, where many very small municipalities believe land-use decisions are theirs alone to make, without regard for any impact beyond their borders.

But collectively, these community-based decisions are having far-reaching effects on the economic and social environment of the entire state and on the greater New England region as well.

Despite the slowdown in population growth, New Hampshire residents continue to see sprawl development use up large tracts of land, increase traffic, and in some places alter the community spirit of their historic and picturesque towns. We should not be surprised when residents react to the effects of residential sprawl by trying to stop or severely restrict further residential development. But this is the wrong course to take.

Rising property taxes have also moved many communities to limit residential growth in the belief that increasing numbers of children are causing their tax bills to rise. But school enrollments have been falling nearly everywhere in the state while at the same time school property taxes have been escalating, for reasons that have nothing to do with the number of children.

The twin perceptions of runaway growth and exploding school enrollments are driving voters and planning boards to place more limits on residential development, especially on types of housing attractive to or affordable for younger or working people. One example is increasing minimum lot sizes, which only enlarges development's footprint and creates more sprawl. Another is giving speedier approval and a warmer welcome to age-restricted housing—the only housing discrimination allowed by law.

Widespread but false perceptions of high growth cloud people's ability to grasp the facts of slowing growth and declining numbers of young people. Voters perceive what they see around them. They focus on any sprawling development. If a couple of families with children move into a neighborhood or some new homes are built nearby, it seems to confirm the perception of an exploding school-age population.

Too often it is affluent families from other states who occupy these homes, contributing to the illusion of burgeoning numbers of school-age children. Communities are not providing housing affordable to their own younger generation. Recent graduates, young professionals, and working families are forced to choose between ever-longer commutes and leaving for other regions with more housing choices and more reasonable costs of living. This pattern of long commutes—45 minutes to an hour—has both environmental and social consequences.

New Hampshire's quality of life, cultural opportunities, and advantageous tax climate have attracted large numbers of maturing baby boomers and retired people. This influx has to a degree camouflaged the exodus of young adults. But New Hampshire and the rest of New England are aging more rapidly than other areas, greatly diminishing the region's prospects for economic growth.

This situation is extraordinary because it is both unintentional and self-induced. Each year in virtually all New Hampshire towns, newcomers and old-timers come together to practice direct democracy through Town Meeting government. This structure of a great many small, local governments with high citizen participation served the state and region quite well for most of the past three centuries.

But the deep-seated culture of local autonomy has allowed each community to favor what it desires for itself, even at the expense of what the state or the local region of communities needs to sustain economic health. When young people are unable to settle and establish families, commitment to community and sense of place are diminished. Something vitally important is lost: social capital.

Social capital is the advantage communities gain from all the vital interrelationships and connections that make a cohesive and successful society. When workers cannot find affordable homes near their jobs and thus must commute long distances, they have much less time and energy for family and community relationships and responsibilities—social capital is lost. When older people are isolated from other age groups and the larger community and see that their children or grandchildren cannot afford to live anywhere near them, still more social capital is lost. Bonds between generations, both within families and within the larger community, are broken. Commitment to public education and to the future declines.

We do not seek villains to blame for the present situation. Rather, this is an account of how people in small towns and cities are making decisions they think are best for themselves without sufficient understanding of the profoundly negative present and long-term consequences.

Fortunately, the unbalancing of New Hampshire's human ecology is happening slowly enough that it can be changed. If people act soon, working together in towns and cities over the next few years, we can avert a very undesirable future.

Our purpose is to raise awareness of the negative outcomes of basing local residential development decisions primarily on one issue—school costs—instead of on the full range of social, economic, and environmental needs and concerns of balanced, vibrant communities.

The other five New England states are experiencing many of the same issues related to local autonomy and the out-migration of young people that we will examine here in New Hampshire, where we live. But New Hampshire towns and cities are under greater pressure because they pay a significantly larger proportion of the costs for public education and other local government functions than do municipalities in other states.

This book explains the changing demography of New Hampshire, its causes and its consequences. Throughout the book and companion documentary are stories of New Hampshire residents of all ages who are struggling with these issues. We also find some answers to how people can start in their own communities to turn this tide. Many of the changes that can help solve our human ecology problems are also good for the environment and for the social fabric of our towns and city neighborhoods.

Our goal is to foster a statewide conversation that will result in greater understanding and motivation to change—to restore generational balance and social capital. If people read this book but fail to take any action to be more welcoming to younger residents, the consequences for our communities and our state will be bleak indeed.

CHAPTER 1

❧ How Did We Get So Gray?

Citizens voting at the budget deliberative session in the Town of Epping

Many people we've talked to at meetings around the state believe New Hampshire's population is growing extremely fast. They believe "out-of-control" growth is causing school enrollments and property-tax bills to "explode." In fact the state's population is growing quite slowly, and more slowly each year. The numbers of children and young adults are on the decline throughout the state,

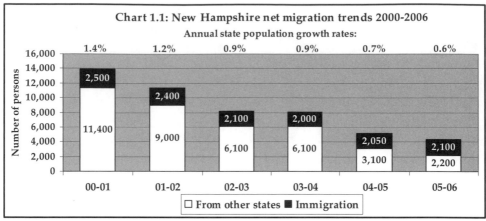

Source: Census Bureau estimates

New Hampshire's population growth is slowing in part because fewer people are moving here from other states.

and the rising older population has vaulted New Hampshire into the ranks of the oldest in the nation.

Year-round-resident growth in New Hampshire, for example, has slowed to 0.6% per year, the highest in New England but well below the national average of 1% per year. New England's annual population growth rate, including New Hampshire, from 2005 to 2006 was a minimal 0.1%, slower than any other region in the nation.

In-migration Has Slowed to a Trickle

Chart 1.1 shows one of the reasons for New Hampshire's slowing growth: fewer people are moving into the state each year from other states, and the relatively small number of immigrants is also down from earlier in the decade.

This trend is a sharp departure from the past. During the 1980s, New Hampshire's population grew at twice the national rate: 20.5% versus the nation's 9.8%, primarily because so many people moved to the state from other parts of the nation. In the 1990s, growth slowed to 11.4%, as opposed to the nation's 13.1%. During the current decade, New Hampshire's population growth is expected to be even slower, about half the nation's projected 10% increase.

Declining "Natural Increase"

The second reason for New Hampshire's slowing population growth is the decline in natural increase—that is, the number of births minus the number of deaths. This results directly from the combined trends of high out-migration of young adults and rapid growth in numbers of older people.

Natural increase in New Hampshire from mid-2005 to mid-2006 added about 3,600 residents. That's down 19% from the 4,400 added between 2000 and 2001. Virtually all the natural increase is occurring in the state's southern counties. Between 2005 and 2006, half the counties in the state—Belknap, Carroll, Coos, Grafton, and Sullivan—actually lost population because there were more deaths than births.

That situation, known as negative natural increase, only occurs when there has been a considerably more rapid than normal aging of the population. That atypical aging pattern is affecting not only New Hampshire, but the rest of New England as well.

Generations Out of Balance

According to the latest U.S. Census Bureau estimates, New Hampshire's median age—the point where half the state's residents are older and half are younger—is now 39.4 years old. To put that in perspective, the state's median age is now three years older than the nation's. New Hampshire now has roughly the same median age as Florida.

It hasn't always been that way.

Back in 1990, New Hampshire had the same median age as the nation and it was three and a half years younger than Florida's. In the intervening years, the altered age distribution of the state has unbalanced New Hampshire's age profile. And as we will see, that has huge long-term consequences.

Here's an illustration of that unbalancing. For every New Hampshire resident age 65 and older in 1990, there were 1.6 young adults 25 to 34 years old. But by 2005, that ratio had dropped precipitously to only 0.9 young adult for every resident age 65 or older. By comparison, that ratio for the country was 1.4 young adults in 1990 and 1.1 young adults in 2005.

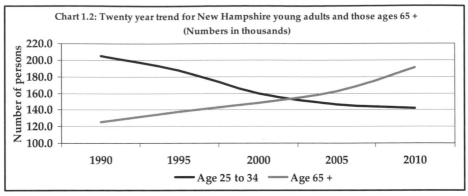

Source: Census Bureau estimates and projections.

The rising count of older residents along with declining numbers of young adults is unbalancing New Hampshire's human ecology.

The combination of senior tax abatements, age-restricted housing, and low state taxes has made New Hampshire, unique among New England states, a magnet for senior citizens. From the 2000 census to mid-2006 there was almost no change (a 0.4% rise) in the age-65-and-older population in the other New England states. That elderly population increased 10% in New Hampshire, however, a gain of nearly 15,000 senior residents versus only about 6,000 in the rest of the region. Nationwide, that same age 65+ cohort rose at a significantly slower rate: 6.5%. All this points to the likelihood that New Hampshire's retirement-age population will grow much faster than can be attributed to just the aging of the baby boomers, the oldest of whom was just 61 years old in 2007.

Young Adults Are Leaving—with Their Born and Unborn Children

In the six years from 2000 to 2006, young adults ages 25 to 34 increased nationwide by over 1%, but fell about 3% in New Hampshire and 9% in the rest of New England, due largely to the departure of so many young people. At the same time, as Chart 1.3 shows, the numbers of children under age 18 have also dropped in New Hampshire and the other New England states, despite rising nationwide.

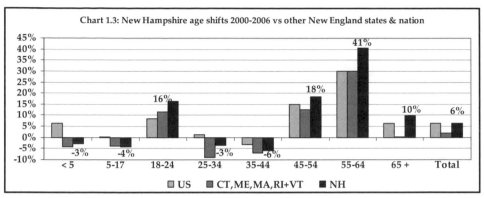

Chart 1.3: New Hampshire age shifts 2000-2006 vs other New England states & nation

Source: Census Bureau estimates

New Hampshire's population is aging more rapidly that other states in part because of higher growth in the population ages 55 or older.

In stark contrast, Chart 1.3 shows New Hampshire's 55-to-64 age cohort growing at a pace considerably faster than that of either the rest of New England or the nation as a whole. This sharp rise may be due in part to past in-migration of baby boomers, but part of the reason may also be the construction of more than 3,500 units of housing in the state, many quite affordable, but restricted to residents ages 55 and older.

College graduates and young professionals enter the workforce here, and elsewhere in America, with sizable debt, and usually start on the lower rungs of the wage and salary ladder. But New Hampshire students finish their bachelor's degrees with the highest average graduating student debt of any state. It's now $22,800, nearly twice the national average of $11,700. While the state proffers carrots for older people, young people get sticks.

Housing affordability—how the cost of renting or buying local homes relates to local wages and salaries—is a big problem for young workers not only in New Hampshire, but also throughout the rest of New England.

New Hampshire's demographic imbalance—a population that is aging more rapidly than normal, combined with exceedingly slow growth and the exodus of too many young people—is depleting the future workforce. If balance is not restored, it will slowly but surely strangle the state's prospects for economic growth.

Big Impacts of a Thousand Little Votes

We find no one cause for this complex condition, and no one person or organization to hold responsible. The causes are more likely to be found in the thousands of decisions—made by state legislators, local planning boards, and voters in hundreds of towns across the state—that make it increasingly expensive for the young to live here, but very economical for the old.

Young adults get a message every time a town or city votes to grant another property-tax break specifically for the elderly, and every time proposed construction of affordable housing open to all receives fierce opposition, just as age-restricted housing gets quick approval. The message for young adults: "We don't want you here because we think that excluding you will lower our property taxes."

Young people have been getting that message for some years now. But they don't vote anywhere nearly as often as older people do. They vote with their feet. They leave for states where financing of public education is primarily a county function, not left to aging and cost-averse property-tax payers in small towns.

Rebalancing the Human Habitat

Communities in New England need the energy, creativity, and idealism of younger workers and citizens. They need all the skills and knowledge of a diverse workforce. The aging baby-boom generation is approaching retirement. Legions of new workers are needed to take their places, and eventually to take care of them.

Young families also support local schools and demand the quality education that is critical to our future and continuing success in this ever-more competitive global economy. A balanced human ecology, with a mix of workers of all ages, is vital to the long-term economic and social health of the entire New England region.

But perceptions that residential growth has no benefit and must be stopped because it will only raise property taxes are widespread.

Once these perceptions take hold in a community, any facts to the contrary are often minimized or ignored. These perceptions, combined with the desire to maintain rising property values, have resulted in many communities prohibiting by various means the creation of any workforce housing. The Workforce Housing Coalition of the Greater Seacoast defines workforce housing as single-family homes, town houses, condominiums, starter homes, and apartments that are affordable to area workers. Residents in many towns and cities are still reacting to perceived high population and household growth during the 1980s construction boom—despite the reality that growth has been declining every year. Watching their rearview mirrors, communities have seen child and young adult populations shrink while the number of residents ages 55 and older has surged.

The precise reasons for the loss of thousands of younger workers and families may vary from more rural and isolated parts of New Hampshire to wealthier, more populated areas, but many of the effects are the same. In the state's northernmost county, Coos, the population of young adults ages 25 to 34 is down 38% since 1990. In the state's richest county, Rockingham, the same age cohort is down 40%. This precipitous drop in the young adult population is not a natural result of a declining birthrate 30 years ago. The missing young adults, many of them well educated and ambitious, have found opportunities and a warmer welcome elsewhere.

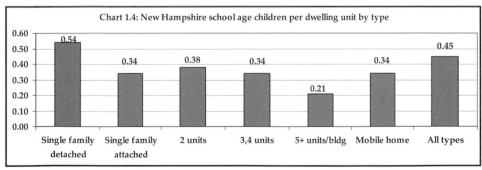

Source: New Hampshire Housing Finance Authority

The myth that every new residence will put two children in local public schools is far from the actual fact.

The Power of Myths

Three persistent myths are factors in effectively discouraging young people from residing in New Hampshire and encouraging retirees and older adults without children to stay here.

Myth one is that for every reasonably affordable unit of work-force housing, two children will attend local schools. Therefore, 100 such units will instantly "flood" the schools with 200 children and drive up property taxes intolerably.

A study commissioned in 2005 by the New Hampshire Housing Finance Authority (*Housing & School Enrollment in NH: An Expanded View*) has shown that each new house results in an average of just one-half child of school age.

Furthermore, no housing development is built all at once. A 100-unit housing development, for example, would take at least four to complete, sell, and fill with residents. That means an average of 20 to 25 occupied units per year.

Thus the reality is that instead of the feared 200 children showing up for school in the fall after the project is approved, 12 or 13 students might be enrolled per year. That's about one child per grade in a K–12 school system, hardly a flood. And during the four- to five-year build-out, at least that number of children will graduate or leave the district. Because enrollment is declining in nearly all school districts,

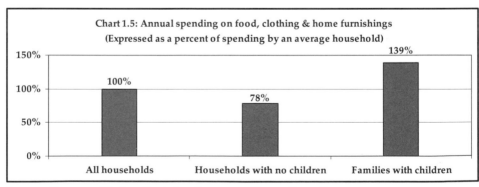

Source: Bureau of Labor Statistics Consumer Expenditure Survey

Retail sales are more negatively affected when the number of families with children declines.

the addition of two or three children per grade will have no impact on property taxes.

Myth number two is that age-restricted housing is a net gain for a town. The idea is that people over age 55 won't put any children in the schools and will make few other demands on the town, so their property taxes are almost all net gain to the town. This thinking also suggests that the net gain will be so large that it will reduce property taxes on present homeowners.

The reality is that older households without children spend far less on food, clothing, and home furnishings at local retail establishments (see Chart 1.5) than do younger families with children. Over time, that lower spending will diminish the value of commercial property, thus lowering the number of such properties and reducing their assessed values—an important component of a town's tax base.

Age-restricted housing also has the effect of unbalancing the normal age distribution of voters, virtually ensuring that warrant articles giving ever larger property tax abatements to senior citizens will be approved, and making it ever more difficult to pass school budgets or muster the two-thirds majority needed to pass school bond issues. The bottom line is that the anticipated property tax "windfall" to towns from permitting large, age-restricted housing developments almost never materializes, and is minimal and short lived if it does.

Myth number three is that what we do in our small town has no effect on the state's economy. In reality, when even small towns prevent the creation of workforce housing or create incentives for retirees, they are contributing to the unbalancing of the human ecology. The impacts of this imbalance affect the economic health not only of the immediate region, but also of the state as a whole.

People making local development and planning decisions must consider the whole picture of social, economic, cultural, and environmental needs and the interests of the community and the larger region. Neighboring towns could better accomplish their goals and serve the needs of the broader community if they worked together more closely.

Sprawl Is the Enemy

Many of the hundreds of thousands of working-age people who moved here over the past 25 years came from heavily populated metropolitan areas in other states. These newer arrivals say openly that they moved here to escape the stress, traffic, and rising cost of living in those heavily populated places. They wish fervently to preserve their new hometown as a low-density, low-tax haven.

These new arrivals—and many longtime residents—tend to equate any workforce housing development with the "uncontrolled sprawl" they chose to escape. In reaction, they often initiate or strongly support the adoption of local regulations to limit and prevent sprawl development, which often have the direct effect of eliminating the creation of more affordable kinds of housing.

Ironically, many of these restrictions are the direct cause of sprawling, land-gobbling patterns of development. Development patterns forced by these restrictive measures end up increasing taxes, too, to pay for maintaining the extra miles of roads, more school busing, and so on.

The answer is reform of local planning regulations to adopt innovative land-use techniques and promote smart-growth patterns of development and resource protection. Chapters 2 and 6 take a closer look at how land-use regulations are connected to lack of affordable housing and to the spread of sprawl.

Tax Haven for Seniors . . .

New Hampshire is highly attractive to people nearing the end of their working lives who want to retire in a state with a low cost of living. It's not difficult to understand why they might want more open space and oppose workforce housing, and favor any housing developments or property-tax abatements designed explicitly for senior citizens.

The point is that many new arrivals come with a mental image of New Hampshire as a low-cost, rural state, and want to keep it that way, at least in their town. Because there are so many very small towns in New Hampshire—most have fewer than 2,000 voters—it's quite

Definition

What Is Workforce Housing?

Workforce housing comprises single-family homes, town houses, condominiums, starter homes, and apartments that are affordable to area workers. One definition of workforce housing is housing that is affordable to households with an income up to 120% of the area's median household income. These income brackets include many people—nurses, teachers, firefighters, police officers, emergency medical service providers, home health care aides, child care providers, farmers and farm workers, carpenters, plumbers, electricians, librarians, landscape professionals and workers, bakers, cooks, chefs, retail workers, government and nonprofit employees, dental hygienists, and technicians of all sorts, for example—who provide the labor and services considered the backbone of any successful community.

possible for relatively few newcomers to become civically active and have a big influence on residential development. This is rarely possible in a metropolitan area.

. . . And Dream Retirement Spot for Boomers

The National Association of Realtors in 2006 conducted a nationwide survey on the retirement preferences of baby boomers, those ages 42 to 60 years.. Nearly two-thirds of respondents said their idea of the perfect place to retire is a "small town or rural area." When they find their ideal place, no one should be surprised that they want to keep it the way they found it.

Many New Hampshire communities support the in-migration of older people by offering them financial incentives that are not available to younger residents. More than 80 towns have housing units that are age-restricted so that no one under age 55 can buy or rent them. Some 100 municipalities offer tax abatements to residents age 65 and older who can demonstrate they have lived in the state for just the past three years and meet a widely varying range of income and asset limits.

These age-preferential provisions were one factor considered by the state Office of Energy and Planning in projecting that the number of people ages 65 to 74 will nearly double (up 86%) in the next 10 years. They project the number of residents ages 35 to 49 to decline by nearly a quarter (24%)—a reduction of over 70,000 people. This represents a critical loss of working-age people and a shrinking of the prime workforce. With the number of empty-nesters rising and the big decrease in adults of parenting age, the number of children—the real future of a community and its workforce—is also projected to decline.

Taken together, the trends of declining numbers of children, rapidly rising cost of public education (see chapter 5), declining numbers of families with school-age children, and rising numbers of older taxpayers with little stake in local schools are simply not sustainable.

The long-term consequences are clear. The Carsey Institute at the University of New Hampshire recently published a paper titled "The Declining Young Adult Population in New England." Author Ross Gittell, a professor at the University of New Hampshire's Whittemore School of Business and Economics, wrote: "[T]he consequences of the demographic changes are substantial . . . the imbalanced growth in the older population leaves the region vulnerable to a host of health and elder care costs without the productive base to support them."

The unbalancing of New Hampshire's human ecology is progressing such that the state's capacity for economic as well as social rejuvenation and vitality is at risk. Unless some generational balance is restored, the state will not be able to meet the 21st-century educational needs of its children, the workforce needs of its industries, or the healthcare needs of the its growing elderly population.

Case in Point

"It's Like You Don't Have Value Until You Own a House"

When people make policies and decisions that affect the ability of young people to live and work in a community, news reporters are often the only ones under 30 in attendance. Most young people don't realize how attitudes and decisions in local communities are limiting their opportunities and options, suggests Larry Clow, a 25-year-old journalist with several year's experience reporting on municipalities large and small.

Larry and a 28-year-old journalist, whom we will call Sophie, have observed local governing bodies and boards making decisions that affect young citizens and their ability to launch careers and establish homes and families.

Between them, Larry and Sophie have covered a range of communities, from the city of Manchester to smaller cities and towns from the North Country to the Seacoast. Both are on the verge of joining the out-migration and bailing out of New Hampshire.

Both of these college-educated professionals agree that many of their peers have left the state for what they see as greener pastures: jobs, economic opportunity, culture, and diversity. There's a sense that the cost of living is too high in relation to wages and salaries for them to ever get ahead in New Hampshire.

Currently based in southeastern New Hampshire, both are frustrated by a lack of living-wage opportunities in publishing. Sophie loves writing and the print media, and she's ambitious. She earned barely $30,000 in 2006. She still owes $10,000 in student loans from her UNH education at in-state tuition rates. Her one-bedroom apartment in a rundown section of a small city costs her $700 month, almost 40% of her after-tax income.

"I feel kind of stuck—living paycheck to paycheck. I just don't see the kind of opportunity I'm looking for in New Hampshire," Sophie says. "My quality of living is subpar; I have higher aspirations."

Larry, on the other hand, loves coastal New England.

"I like New Hampshire a lot," says Larry. "I can see myself—maybe in 10 years—settling down in the state. But right now, I'm missing the cultural stuff." A movie buff, Larry points out that he has to drive to Boston or wait for the DVDs to see any films besides the majors playing in all the local megaplexes.

"For young people, we like places where we can meet other people," Sophie says. "When you get out of work here at 11:30 on Saturday nights, you have no options."

"The demographics on the Seacoast are skewing to older people," Larry says. "And that's what the economy is catering to." He says he can see short-term business gain from marketing to older clientele, but not long term. "Older people are not spending as much money downtown, and so on, as younger people," he observes. And young people will only increase their spending levels as they furnish homes and raise families.

"Younger people are underestimated for what we can contribute, and for what communities can gain from us," Larry says. "When you're a kid, the community views you as a burden on the school system. Then you go to college, and you're viewed as a potential troublemaker. . .

"It's like you don't have value until you own a house," says Larry. The area's high housing costs make it difficult for young people in teaching, firefighting, journalism, and countless other trades and professions to picture themselves owning a home.

"I think these communities are missing out," Larry says. "They should be promoting affordable apartments in town and attracting young people and families. But planning boards don't want kids because of taxes. They don't want anything different in town."

Young adults are ready to take their places as workers and members of the community, but there seems to be no room for them. "It's not like there's a conspiracy against young people," Sophie says. She blames stereotypes. She believes people are thinking and acting in what they perceive is their self-interest, but will eventually regret the lack of generational balance and diversity in their communities.

Sophie recalls a poignant debate when she was reporting on a zoning proposal to ban mobile home or manufactured housing parks in a town in northern New Hampshire: "Just one person stood up and said, 'You're all snobs! Where are young people going to live and get a start in housing?'"

These reporters see devaluation of young people on a collision course with the inflating cost of land and housing. "There's less incentive to give or sell land to the younger generation, because it is worth too much," Sophie says.

She and Larry would like to see towns and cities encourage development of more affordable housing—including starter homes and apartments. They worry about Dover's waterfront redevelopment, for example, which is geared toward luxury condos and high-end retail. Rising downtown rents are driving out retail stores and restaurants in favor of law offices and tax-accounting firms that Larry says will contribute little energy or atmosphere to the downtown. Dover, as one last place in the Seacoast that's not overly gentrified, appeals more to younger people.

Sophie and Larry agree that younger people need to get involved. Most people serving on boards and committees are older and have money, they note, and may not have the interests of younger people at the front of their minds. Towns and cities ought to reach out to younger residents, they conclude.

CHAPTER 2

🌿 Local Concerns vs. Regional Needs

Citizens raising their hands to speak at a Jackson town meeting

Concentration of power in small, local jurisdictions of both municipal and school government is affecting the generational tilt, lack of affordable housing, and sprawl development patterns in several interrelated ways. Costs of schools and other municipal services are higher in many places than they might be with more regional cooperation. Voters have reacted to rapidly rising property taxes by trying to zone children out of any new development. They have enacted development regulations that drive up housing costs, prevent coordination of sewage-treatment systems and transportation-oriented planning, and use up more land for each new home built—all without regard for the social, economic, and environmental impacts on the larger region or state.

Town and city governments in New Hampshire trace their broad powers and authority to the political organization established in 17th-century colonial New England. New England states lack strong county administrative systems as well as the large special districts with authority over narrow public services that typify other regions.

Small School Districts, Big Costs

Most significantly for property taxes, New England distributes school costs and decision making over smaller school districts compared to other regions, which more often administer and fund education at the county level. New England states are also far more dependent on property taxes to fund local government and services. Each of New Hampshire's 234 towns and cities must raise the bulk of what it spends to educate children and youth by taxing land and buildings within the borders of the town. Public education in New Hampshire is governed by local or cooperative school districts, based on the same political boundaries as towns and cities.

Voters in two or more towns may elect to form a cooperative district to provide for education of some or all of the towns' students. When towns form cooperative agreements, they negotiate how costs will be apportioned among taxpayers of the member towns.

State law requires all school districts to form school administrative units (SAUs) to hire a superintendent of schools and staff to provide supervisory administration. The size of the approximately 90 SAUs varies greatly, as do their amount and valuation of taxable property.

The state's largest city, Manchester, is also the state's largest school district and school administrative unit (SAU #37). The city has about 110,000 residents and just over 17,000 students. But most New Hampshire SAUs have fewer than 2,000 students. Many towns and smaller cities have formed joint SAUs to improve financial efficiency, expand expertise, and coordinate curricula among towns served by common middle and/or high schools. But many towns have chosen to go it alone with a one-district SAU.

In a recent example, Barnstead voted to break away from a small, two-town SAU it had with Pittsfield. Both towns are about the same size, with 1,700 households each. Barnstead has a K–12 enrollment of only about 550 students, unchanged since 2000. It leaves Pittsfield with a current enrollment of only 700—a decline of 17% since 2000. It is a virtual certainty that both towns will end up spending far more for public education even with no increase in the number of students.

School Enrollments Falling, Per-Pupil Costs Rising

Regardless of size, more than two-thirds of New Hampshire school administrative units have seen enrollments decline over the past six

Table 1: K–12 Enrollment, Residents Ages 55+ & All Ages: Percent Change 2000–2006			
County	K–12 Enrollment	Residents Ages 55+	All Residents Ages
Belknap	1.7%	20.1%	9.3%
Carroll	-7.3%	16.4%	8.7%
Cheshire	-7.6%	17.9%	4.8%
Coos	-8.0%	7.3%	-0.3%
Grafton	-5.6%	21.7%	4.4%
Hillsborough	1.5%	24.3%	5.8%
Merrimack	-0.8%	23.1%	8.7%
Rockingham	0.3%	31.8%	6.8%
Strafford	-0.4%	19.2%	6.9%
Sullivan	-6.5%	13.9%	6.2%
NH Total	-0.8%	23.0%	6.4%

Source: Census Bureau and N.H. Department of Education

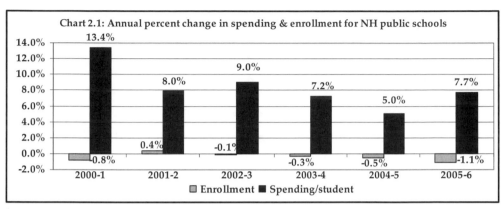

Source: New Hampshire Department of Education

Despite declining enrollments spending on public education in New Hampshire has risen each year since 2000 at above the rate of inflation.

years. As school administrators have long known, when enrollments decline, per-pupil costs rise.

Table 1 shows the surprising truth: despite population growth in nine out of ten New Hampshire counties since 2000, K–12 public school enrollments have declined in all but three counties. Yet the perception persists that building any new homes will cause hikes in both school enrollments and property taxes.

The double-digit growth rate in number of residents ages 55 or older in all but one New Hampshire county may explain why people perceive rapid growth in their communities. On average throughout the state, the age-55-plus population is rising at more than three times the rate of total resident growth. The age-55-plus rate of growth is highest in those counties where the most age-restricted housing has been built.

Chart 2.1 shows that over the past six years, the number of children in New Hampshire public schools has fallen in every year but one. Yet education spending increased an average 7% per year. During this period, the annual rate of inflation averaged less than 3% and never exceeded 3.4%. Thus, every year the cost of public education in New Hampshire rises faster than inflation even though there are no more children to educate than there were six years ago. This pattern of sharply rising property taxes to finance public education for a shrinking number of students is not sustainable in the long term as a matter of public policy.

Twin fears: Increasing Taxes, Declining Property Values

Planning boards around the state are confronted with this perception of runaway school enrollments with every proposal for new residential construction. Fear of families with children—and rising property taxes—drives the debate. Types of housing that might qualify as "affordable" are doubly spurned. Many residents translate lower or affordable sale prices as lower assessments. They envision excess costs of school and other municipal services that will be shifted onto existing homeowners' tax bills.

Residents also express fears that lower-cost or smaller homes will depress overall property values—or at least not contribute to the desired increases of home prices. Homeowners who are really concerned about their property values should pay attention. If allowed to continue, the exodus of younger generations will leave the state with a depressed economy, burdensome healthcare costs, and long-term falling home prices, as it has in other states with similar out-migration patterns.

Widespread declining school enrollments testify to the success of residents of New Hampshire cities and towns in limiting development of single- and multifamily homes in affordable price ranges. A host of measures—growth-control ordinances, large-lot zoning, impact fees, buying up developable land for conservation, plus an array of expensive restrictions and requirements on new construction, from wide roads to occupancy permits—have effectively priced many young people and families with children out of the housing market. Even renting is prohibitively expensive in many communities.

Age-Discriminatory Housing

Construction of age-restricted housing has become a popular response for communities and developers. Existing residents feel virtuous about allowing housing to be built for seniors, while ensuring no children will be added to the school system. Developers like the ease of approval compared to any other—that is, nondiscriminatory—form of housing. Some 55-and-up housing developments have been "affordable," but many are not. Many are luxury units with amenities desired by affluent newcomers, either retired or nearing retirement.

Some claim that mature empty-nesters will sell their larger homes in the community to move into the new seniors-only developments, freeing up older housing stock for younger buyers. But many age-restricted units are filled by retirees or near-retirees attracted from other states or regions.

Until late 2006, no one knew how many age-restricted dwelling units were being built in the state. The New Hampshire Housing Finance Authority (NHHFA) funded a survey conducted by the state's regional planning agencies to find out. That survey found that from 2000 to mid-2006, approximately 3,500 units had been either built or permitted.

Nearly three-quarters of those units (73%) were located in Hillsborough and Rockingham Counties—despite the fact that those two counties have 53% of all the residents in the state and less than half (48%) of households occupied by people ages 55 or older. Some of the highest home prices in the state are found in these two counties, reflecting the strong demand for housing. Yet during this same period, only 42% of all non-age-restricted housing units permitted or built in the state were in the communities of Rockingham and Hillsborough counties.

It's the Sprawl, Not the People

Some opposition to growth is rooted in a desire to protect environmental quality and the signature character of New Hampshire towns and landscape. These are legitimate concerns. But the negative environmental and community impacts of development in recent years is less a factor of increasing numbers of people and homes than of the sprawling nature of residential and commercial development. Consumption of land for development has far exceeded actual growth in population.

New approaches to community and regional planning, such as Smart Growth and New Urbanism, show that population growth does not have to ruin traditional communities and landscapes. It is possible to accommodate and gain economic vitality from continuing growth, at the same time maintaining the character and quality of life that make New Hampshire such a desirable place to live, work, and visit. Residents appreciate New Hampshire as a great place to raise a family or start a business—because of its strong communities and ethic of independence and civic responsibility.

Fearing the loss of their community's character and scenic landscape to cookie-cutter commercial strip-development and look-alike subdivisions, many residents vehemently oppose any new development in their neighborhoods and towns. The rapid growth experienced in some parts of the state in the 1980s left many people feeling a sense of loss and resistant to further change. Instead of welcoming the positive economic opportunities afforded by growth and change, many residents fear growth will lead to loss of control and loss of traditional small-town New England character.

"A Consensus of Hope"

These understandable fear reactions are behind many well-intentioned efforts to regulate growth. But the law of unintended consequences has brought about the opposite effect. The resulting regulations have proved to be blueprints for sprawl. In his book *Home from Nowhere: Remaking Our Everyday World for the 21st Century,* James Howard Kunstler argues that the existing consensus of fear that has shaped zoning and development regulations is not a sound basis for regulating development. "We need a consensus of hope," he proposes.

Most master plans pay homage to the traditional character of a community, but most zoning ordinances prohibit the traditional patterns of development that created that cherished character. The compact, walkable, denser settlement patterns of New Hampshire city and town centers are enviably livable. The traditional development patterns of places like Portsmouth and Peterborough were established long before zoning was invented.

Downtowns and village centers were developed around a mix of land uses: community institutions and public buildings, a variety of businesses and offices, and diverse types of residences from stately homes to small apartments. Surrounding environs of more rural farms, forests, and less densely built homes and businesses offered variety and relief, and provided for other land-use and resource needs.

New Hampshire residents are correct in perceiving that sprawl development has been eating away at their treasured landscape. In the 15 years from 1982 to 1997, for example, the Manchester Nashua metropolitan area population grew by 28%. But urbanized land area increased by a whopping 70%, which resulted in a 25% decline in population density. The Portsmouth-Dover-Rochester metro area experienced the similar loss of density that comes with sprawl. The area actually became 25% less dense because although the number of residents increased by 32%, the urbanized area grew at more than twice that rate, expanding by 76%!

Some argue that builders are simply responding to market demands for larger, more-expensive homes on larger lots. Another NHHFA study found that new housing construction has indeed been concentrated in the moderate-high to high-priced categories, as opposed to the moderate and lower prices needed by much of the state's workforce. However, lower-to-moderate-price homes have appreciated in value at faster rates than high-end homes—indicating greater, unmet demand.

Preservation vs. Workforce Housing

Here's what often happens when a housing development is proposed in a town. A developer will propose a plan to build 90 homes on 300 acres of open land—in conformance with the town's three-acre minimum zoning. Individuals opposed to that wasteful use of the land rally support for buying up all 300 acres for permanent conservation as open space. Federal and state grants are obtained and combined with a town bond issue to purchase the land, and the development is stopped.

Housing in that town—and neighboring towns—becomes more expensive because the supply has been constricted and growth slows. Proponents of preserving open space primarily to avoid tax increases do not take into account these long-term consequences of artificially constricting residential growth.

Instead, the town could insist on a more innovative and creative approach that would allow more concentrated development—perhaps even a multiple-use village development with workforce housing—on the portion of that 300-acre parcel that offered the easiest transportation access and the least environmental impact. The 90 homes, or combination of homes and businesses, could be clustered on 50 acres or so to create a true, and more traditional, neighborhood. Much of the remaining 200 to 250 acres could be permanently preserved as recreation and/or conservation land. The more compactly built homes would be far more affordable to working and younger people. Each unit would contribute to the costs of providing municipal services. And the town would also get new park and/or conservation land.

Local desires to preserve open space rather than permit a workforce housing development may arise because the land in question is valuable farmland or contains exceptional wildlife habitat and has been designated in the master plan as a priority for conservation. But too often the push to preserve open space or prevent development has more to do with newer residents who fear that any development will transform their neighborhood into the sprawling congestion they fled elsewhere. And many opponents are motivated by the desire to limit the number of families with children.

What Is a Hometown?

It has become increasingly difficult—in many areas nearly impossible—for young people to buy, or even rent, places to live in or near the towns where they grew up and went to school. Uprooting of young people starting out in life separates them from their support networks of people and institutions. It breaks down the complex multigenerational relationships that have characterized small-town and neighborhood economic, cultural, and social life. It erodes the traditional New England values of civic commitment and service. The middle and older generations have less of an investment in the community when they see little chance that their children or grandchildren will find a place to settle and raise their own families.

An Unnatural Deviation

The demographic shift in New Hampshire and indeed the rest of New England—the exodus of young adults and the influx of residents over 55—is not natural. The rapid graying of the region, the shrinking numbers of young adults and children accompanied by the rapid rise in numbers of older people, is driven by local residential development policies. The facts are quite stark: slowing growth, rising out-migration of younger adults, and an increasing number of older adults mean a fast-aging population with fewer children.

The more affluent families with children who are able to afford local homes typically come from other states. But the influx of these affluent parents has slowed, and is not enough to keep school enrollments even steady in most communities. Public schools are projected to decline even further over the next decade. Experience shows that declining enrollments can be even more expensive for school districts to manage than growth.

By turning away the young, the state and its communities will soon cause workforce shrinkage, resulting in dramatically slower economic growth. But citizens cannot be blamed entirely for voting in their short-term self-interest, even at the price of longer-term detriment.

Education costs at all levels, and across the nation, have been rising for decades at rates well above inflation. The traditional New England government and taxation patterns were established centuries ago, and for an agrarian society. It's no wonder people in many situations chafe at their property-tax bills. Those who have owned a home or land in a town for a long time may not have the income to match the spiraling costs of paying for municipal and educational expenses in a community with rising expectations for services. Older residents—newcomers or not—are less willing to make sacrifices for local education costs when they know their grandchildren will never attend local schools. Adding insult to injury, property-tax bills come in one or two huge bites a year, unlike easier-to-swallow taxes that are deducted in small increments from paychecks or counted in pennies added to purchases.

New Hampshire's heavy reliance on local property taxes has aggravated the problem. But we don't believe that a new tax structure is necessary to address the problem of out-migrating young adults. We do believe that changing local zoning and planning practices is very necessary, and increasing regional collaboration would help a lot. But making communities more welcoming to young families may ultimately come down to a fundamental attitude shift such that children are once again viewed as a vital community resource, and not just an intolerable financial burden.

Case in Point I

Large-lot Mania vs. Open-space Conservation Development

Communities vote to mandate ever-increasing lot size as a "knee-jerk reaction to growth," says Mike DiBitetto, a civil engineer and six-year town councilor in Hooksett. "People imagine that if you double lot size, you will halve the growth." Increasing lot size fails to affect rate of population growth. Instead, it accelerates the rate of land development.

Requiring bigger lots is counterproductive, DiBitetto says. The result is the maxed-out checkerboards of suburban development so familiar to frequent flyers. "Every Smart Growth and New Urbanism planning study tells you not to expand lot size. The way to preserve more open space is to increase density," he says.

"We need to come to grips—a backyard acre of grass for every house is not the same value as contiguous open space with some natural environment." It's not just Hooksett, adds the frustrated DiBitetto: "I haven't seen any community embrace Smart Growth as a solution." He focuses his land-planning and development activities outside of Hooksett to avoid conflicts of interest.

Zoning ordinances have become so complex and unwieldy that they rule out creativity in designing the best development for a specific parcel of land, argues DiBitetto, who is also a former Hooksett planning board member. "They tend to force a certain uniformity—not good, unless you want sameness."

Hooksett has a cluster, or open-space conservation, subdivision zoning provision. Planning board members, like those in many other towns, wonder why few such density-gaining, open-space conserving plans are proposed. "It's a painful process," says DiBitetto, who has worked with Randall Arendt, the noted conservationist and land designer. "The most punitive regulations relate to cluster." Punish developers, he says, and "you'll get less." Most towns' cluster ordinances do not offer enough incentives or density bonuses, while requiring "more hoops to jump through" he says.

Randall Arendt has written what he describes as a constructive critique of outmoded subdivision ordinance provisions. "Flawed Processes, Flawed Results, and a Potential Solution" and other articles are available on his firm's Web site www.greeenerprospects.com. Arendt details weaknesses common to many open-space subdivision regulations. He says the first step should be identifying land areas to be preserved, preferably in concert with a town-wide map of potential conservation land. Then homes should be sited to take best advantage of those protected lands—as neighborhood squares, village greens, commons, playing fields, greenways, farmland, or forest preserves.

Arendt argues that the two greatest weaknesses of most open-space subdivision regulations are failure to define open space in this manner and requiring excessive buffers around cluster subdivisions, "as if it were a gravel pit, junkyard, or leper colony," he writes.

DiBitetto finds that most towns require deeper buffers for cluster subdivisions than for conventional apartment developments or commercial sites. These regulations not only counteract the goals of open-space subdivision ordinances, but they also increase the costs and reduce the numbers of homes that can be built.

Fear drives these regulatory attempts to close every possible loophole—and to limit construction of homes because of school costs.

"I like the town meeting—the purest form of democracy— but it tends to look inward," DiBitetto says, "not looking to see what your neighbor towns are doing." He thinks the state needs to look at growth patterns and stress more conformity to overall master plans. "Otherwise," he says, "every town shuts the door and pushes it to the next town."

Case in Point II

Fight for a New Neighborhood and Community in Deerfield

Gina and Jeff White had long planned to subdivide their property in Deerfield, New Hampshire, to finance their two sons' college education. They purchased their home and 160 acres of land in 1993. Since then they also bought an abutting 90-acre parcel with a gravel pit. Their older son, at 19, has started college, and his brother is now 16. But the Whites' plan to develop the land around their home into a family-welcoming neighborhood has sparked conflict at every step.

Abutters immediately rallied with petitions to stop any sort of growth, claiming subdivision of the Whites' property would be detrimental to the town. Citizens, including some local officials, opposed the plan, claiming that school enrollments and taxes would go up and land in open space would go down.

Gina says other owners of large parcels of land became alarmed by some opponents' talk of using eminent domain to stop the subdivision. "They showed little regard for property owners or their personal investment in the land," she says. At this writing, the town stands divided.

Both Whites come from a working-class background. A 41-year-old writer and homemaker, Gina was born and raised in Manchester. Jeff, 49, came to New Hampshire from Gloucester, Massachusetts, 30 years ago. He is a builder and small-scale developer, constructing three or four houses a year in southern New Hampshire.

The Whites feel fortunate. Their business has done well. Gina, who loves animals, has some horses. She loves their land with its views of Saddleback Mountain and the Pawtuckaways. The Whites want to share those views—but not just with people who can pay half a million dollars for the kind of house typically built in Deerfield these days.

Deerfield is a rural town of nearly 3,700 inhabitants in the northwestern corner of Rockingham County. Still heavily forested, it contains portions of Pawtuckaway and Bear Brook State Parks on the east and west ends of town and historic village centers in between.

"We moved here for the tight-knit community," says Gina, who has enjoyed volunteering in the local school. Jeff coaches baseball. "We loved the welcomed feeling we received from the good-hearted New England people who lived here at the time."

But rising real-estate prices have brought dramatic change to Deerfield. "Very upper-end people from the city have moved in," Gina explains, "and have forced others out."

Selectman Andy Robertson is also disturbed by the changes in the town's character that seem to come with its new demographic profile. "We've been talking as selectmen," says the 43-year-old father of two. "More and more, people in their 50s and 60s, or just-retired folks, have moved here from elsewhere. They're not interested in the schools—or about anything [else] in the community except ambulances."

Robertson describes the typical new residents as 59-year-old CEOs or high-level executives from Massachusetts or Connecticut who retired early. "They keep repeating their mantra," he says with frustration, against any development that might bring children and raise tax bills.

"There's a strong conservation movement in Deerfield," Robertson says, and he, counts himself in that camp. But he says conservation of rural quality and open space "has just been commandeered" in opposition to any new homes that might be occupied by families with school-aged children. He's sympathetic to the Whites, describing their proposal as "a responsible, progressive plan."

The Whites express great pride in their open-space cluster development plan, with its winding roads and beautiful views. One hundred acres with the best mountain views will be permanently protected for conservation. "Some of the house lots will also have views of Fort Mountain," Gina adds. "The subdivision has been designed as a family-friendly community, with access to walking trails through forests of pines, oak, birch, hemlock, beech, and yellow birch."

In short, the Whites have designed the kind of neighborhood they would choose for themselves, the kind of community they envision for their future grandchildren. They have reserved two lots for their sons to build homes someday.

The Whites also donated 11 acres of land to the town to create new ball fields. Jeff and Gina see the fields as an asset for the town and for the families who will live in or near the subdivision. But even the donated fields drew attacks from residents who don't have children, including a planning board member who worried about the minimal tax impact of future field maintenance.

"The abutters don't like the playing fields, even though the town has dire need of field space," Gina says. They don't want the kids and the traffic of people bringing kids for games or practice. Some newer town residents send their children to private schools, she says, and "have nothing to do with the community. You're not seeing the family values we used to have."

Many opponents did not want development of any sort. Newspaper accounts of various planning board and other public meetings report the numerous questions and objections raised about children and school enrollment. But the loudest opposition is over the Whites' goal of qualifying at least 15 of the 50 houses as affordable by the standards of the New Hampshire Housing Finance Authority.

Jeff and Gina White are intensely concerned about the unavailability of affordable housing in their community, and are trying to do something about it. "A lot of the kids who have grown up here want to come back after college—and they can't," they say. "Our older son says he wants to raise his family here."

Deerfield residents Joe and Noreen Dubiansky worry that their own sons, a technical worker and a teacher both in their 20s, can't afford to live on their own in town. The older son is a volunteer firefighter and EMT. Joe, an attorney whose office is also in Deerfield, has begun to speak up for families and for affordable housing choices at public meetings. "Both of our sons seem to want to live in Deerfield. That's what brought it home to me. It's hard to even find an apartment that's affordable," Joe says.

Joe recalls renting an apartment with roommates when he came to town nearly 40 years ago. He and Noreen bought a piece of land in 1975 and began building their home, which they lived in through various stages of construction. "We all started that way back then," he says. Occupancy permitting regulations preclude that option in most towns today.

A former planning board member, Joe Dubiansky notes that Deerfield has focused on cluster development: "But when you add all the regulations together, it's not easier to make affordable housing." The same density rules apply, making it hard to build lower-priced homes.

"And it's very difficult to build any kind of multifamily housing," he adds.

"Unless there is some kind of tax advantage for affordable or workforce housing like there is for elderly housing, which seems to work quite well, it's going to be a long haul in New Hampshire," Joe Dubiansky says. "New Hampshire Housing Finance Authority assistance for people under their guidelines is all we have."

The Whites have discussed their project with NHHFA to make sure their more affordable units will qualify. Some people in town were shocked to learn that homes in the $260,000 to $285,000 range are considered "affordable," and that families earning up to $81,000 a year can qualify for financing assistance. But those prices are significantly lower than those of homes currently offered in Deerfield. And it points up just how much people must earn to buy a home in this and other communities.

The Whites would prefer to build all the houses in the entry-level range, but without help from the town, many will be priced at $350,000 to $400,000. Even without help from the town, Gina vows they will keep as many houses in the affordable range as they can. "We hope to get some down to $260,000—for three-bedroom, 1.5-bath homes."

Joe Dubiansky points out that young people starting out are not the only ones hurt by lack of affordable housing choices. In his law practice, he sees many divorcing couples struggle to hold on to a home. Many divorcing parents want to live in the same town as their children. In most cases in southern New Hampshire, that just isn't possible, he says, to the detriment of the families.

"I think, as much as I can appreciate what is available for the aging population," says the 60-year-old Dubiansky, "some of these towns in southeastern New Hampshire are going to be made up of a mostly aging population. A vital town is one that has young kids, young couples, young single people."

Despite the opposition to development, Deerfield still has leaders and residents who envision a community that includes people of all ages and walks of life. They believe in and are fighting to rebuild the close intergenerational ties, traditional values, and neighborly cooperation of their New England town.

CHAPTER 3

🦋 Thumb on the Scale

Aerial view showing a less developed part of the Town of Deerfield

Many communities have embraced age-restricted residential development as a way of keeping a lid on property taxes. The intent is clear, as these developments limited to people ages 55 or 62 and up are often referred to as "childproof" housing. In some towns, the only affordable housing tolerated by town residents is that which is restricted to people 55 and up. As noted in chapter 2, the age-55-plus rate of growth is highest in those counties where the most age-restricted housing has been built.

"New Hampshire's heavy and growing reliance on property taxes creates a financial challenge for homeowners with modest incomes, particularly if their incomes are fixed or falling. Lower-income retirees are one group that may experience a cash flow problem when property taxes are due." So noted a 2005 report from the New Hampshire Center for Public Policy Studies titled "Shifting the Load." The state, municipalities, and federal government have all created a variety of programs to reduce seniors' property-tax bill, or to help them use the equity in their homes to pay their taxes.

But New Hampshire's property-tax exemptions for seniors, the study noted, have the drawback of shifting costs onto other property-tax payers, including those with even lower incomes but who happen to be under age 65.

Preferential Tax Treatment Is a Thumb on the Scale

New Hampshire law requires towns to give exemptions to senior homeowners who meet certain income and asset criteria: income of less than $13,400 for a single homeowner; less than $20,400 for a married couple; and assets of less than $35,000—excluding the value of the home and at least two acres. But the law authorizes towns to increase the level of relief beyond the statutory minimum by vote of local legislators.

Based on 2003 information, the "Shifting the Load" study found that 47 communities were using the state's minimum income limits and 79 had kept the asset limits. But most communities have adopted much higher limits, granting tax exemptions to more seniors with more income and greater assets. In 2003, towns had raised income limits to as high as $50,000 and $60,000. The state's median household income that year was $55,166. Many towns use a limit of $40,000 per couple, which is 73% of the state's median household income. Thus, many towns have voted to provide tax exemptions to seniors with incomes that would be considered moderate—in fact, quite typical of the state as a whole. Towns with the highest income limits actually exceed the state's median income. This means younger taxpayers are subsidizing tax bills of older residents in the wealthier half of the population.

Most towns used the state minimum asset limit of $35,000, but as of 2003 three towns (Candia, Chester, and Litchfield) had granted tax breaks to seniors with up to $300,000 in assets. And Hooksett had no limit on the homeowners' assets. By law, the asset limits do not include the value of a taxpayer's home. Older taxpayers who want to hide assets can make out quite well.

The "Shifting the Load" report concluded that senior property-tax abatement programs are growing rapidly, "as is the proportion of New Hampshire residents over the age of 65, heightening the need to attend to the impact of tax shifting at the local level."

Chart 3.1 shows the growth in senior tax abatements since 2000. By 2005 those abatements had risen 61%, and are undoubtedly more than $20 million today.

If municipalities continue to respond to the pressure of escalating taxes "by exempting more and more seniors from ever larger portions of the tax burden, they will necessarily be increasing the

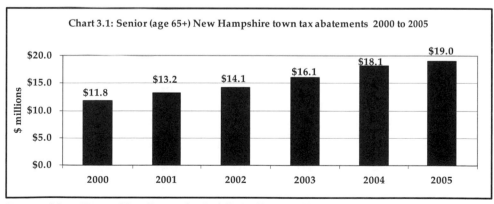

Source: New Hampshire Center for Public Policy Studies

Property tax abatements for seniors in New Hampshire increased at a compound annual rate of 10% per year from 2000 to 2005.

pressure on other taxpayers, regardless of their income or ability to pay," says the report. If something doesn't change, conflict over rising property taxes and how the burden will be distributed is likely to drive an increasingly contentious wedge between generations.

Shrinking Workforce Is Already a Drag on Economy

"Portsmouth is a case study in these demographic trends. It's an incredible challenge for the city," says Portsmouth's exasperated Director of Economic Development Nancy Carmer. The diverse character of its population is what has made Portsmouth such an interesting city historically, she adds. Artists, people who made their living from the sea and workers in the city's maritime industries all lived in the city.

"It's getting hard to draw companies here, when there is not the workforce," says Carmer, whose job is to lure businesses to the city to expand its property-tax base.

That's the irony: the lack of workers and the kinds of housing they could afford is driving away the very businesses that could lift some of the property-tax burden from homeowners. Yet residents continue to vote down efforts to increase the variety and supply of less expensive homes out of fear their taxes will go up.

Carmer notes that Portsmouth had the opportunity in 2007 during the base-closure process to acquire and rehab the Doble Army Reserve Center as workforce housing. The 3.4-acre site is located off the Route 1 Bypass, near the Pease International Tradeport and its nearly 7,000 jobs.

The city council debated between municipal and housing uses of the property. At a public hearing, many neighbors spoke in opposition to the housing proposal. They especially opposed workforce housing. Subsequently, the council rejected the housing plan, voting 8-1 in favor of using the property for recreational or police purposes.

Yet the most pressing concerns voiced by businesses of all sizes and types at roundtables held around the state by the Business and Industry Association, Carmer points out, are the costs of health care and workforce housing.

On a personal level, too, Carmer understands the impacts of the lack of affordable housing. Like much of the city's workforce, she and her husband cannot afford to live in Portsmouth, and must join the twice-daily crush of commuter traffic on the Spaulding Turnpike. They live in Rollinsford, a slightly more affordable community about 12 miles to the north.

But Rollinsford is no solution for today's younger generation, as larger, more- expensive houses are increasingly the rule there, too. "I have children now starting college," Carmer says. With rising housing costs throughout the region, she worries about what opportunities they will have: "They don't seem to want to go very far away, but will they ever be able to come back here to live?" she worries.

Carmer worries that the growing income inequality is irreparably tearing the social warp and weft of New Hampshire Seacoast communities, and of towns throughout the rest of New England. "Generations can't live here anymore," she says.

How Many Miles to the Servants' Quarters?

Stratham's Town Planner Chuck Grassie says his family struggles with launching their young adult children in this high-cost housing environment. "I see what our own children go through because of the lack of affordable housing," says Grassie, who lives in Rochester. One son has returned from serving in Iraq.

Higher costs, and the kinds of zoning and regulations that force up costs, are reaching farther and farther out from the Seacoast, Grassie notes: "Even Wakefield [a small community 47 miles north in Carroll County] now has a two- or three-acre minimum lot size. . . .

"We do need to provide housing for all facets of the population," Grassie says. He wrestles with these issues in Stratham, the affluent Seacoast town of about 7,000 residents, where he works, and in Rochester, where he lives and is an elected member of the city council. Considered a more affordable community for people working in the Seacoast, Rochester is the state's fourth largest city with a population of 31,000.

Stratham does not have a reputation as an affordable community. The approximate one-third of town staff that live in Stratham are mostly longtime residents. The joke around the municipal offices is that Stratham is a gated community—and town employees are the servants who lock the gates when they go home at night.

Wages earned by many Seacoast workers should be a reality check for people who think workforce housing is unnecessary in these communities. "Many jobs that require a college education pay $10 an hour or less. Many other jobs—certified nurse's aides, for example—start at $7.50," Grassie says. "We recently had a young engineer trying to find a place [and] he needed something less than a $188,000 condo."

"Not In My Back Yard—NIMBY—is the biggest problem for workforce housing," Grassie says. Over his career in city government and as a planner, Grassie has attended countless meetings and hearings on proposals to add affordable housing provisions to zoning ordinances, or for development proposals featuring affordable housing.

"The first words out of their mouths are 'We don't want that kind of people here,' " Grassie says. "It's a form of cultural and economic racism. They are the people you see every day—making your change, taking care of your kids or your grandparent."

When the Workforce Housing Coalition and a Seacoast developer proposed a development in Rochester, Grassie spoke in favor of the project. The proposed homes were moderate-not low-income housing, priced at $150,000 to $200,000. Still, neighbors reacted negatively.

"This was workforce housing—for police, teachers, employees of local businesses," Grassie says. "These were exactly the people who lived in the neighborhood, yet they all came and said, 'We don't want those kinds of people living here.' "

Grassie heard the same language at Stratham hearings on a proposed ordinance to include workforce housing in a small redevelopment district. Residents made it clear: affordable housing anywhere in town would be acceptable only if it was restricted to people ages 55 or older.

Watch That Cost-shifting

This perception, that age-restricted housing is far preferable to any housing that might increase the number of school-age children, ignores the growing senior property- tax abatements that such developments bring. As more age-restricted housing is permitted, it is reasonable to expect that older homeowners will vote in favor of increasing their abatements, thus shifting still more of the total property-tax burden to younger homeowners.

So far, that nearly $20 million in shifted tax obligations is concentrated in the southern part of the state. In towns like Exeter that have concentrations of older residents, the costs shifted to the rest of the taxpayers are becoming quite significant. But speaking or voting against granting or expanding senior tax abatements is like opposing motherhood and apple pie.

The population age 65 or older in New Hampshire increased only 10% from 2000 to 2005. But the projected jump of 51% by 2015 makes it a safe bet that with continuing preferences for age-restricted housing, senior property-tax abatements will grow much larger. Age-based abatements may end up costing towns a lot more than any workforce housing development.

We're Caught in a Trap

We in New Hampshire are in what psychologists call a social trap—a situation where people in a community take actions to obtain short-term individual gains but which lead in the long run to a loss for the group as a whole. The social trap manifests itself here in the widespread desire to prohibit workforce housing and exclude children from the community, in a futile effort to limit property-tax increases. But this phenomenon is relatively recent.

Whatever Happened to Family Values?

Sometime during the past decade or two, despite all the talk about family values, there was a huge shift in a key public attitude. Young families with children slid from being highly esteemed as essential to our communities' future to near-pariahs as intolerable financial burdens on communities. That change in attitude has profoundly negative economic and social consequences that will play out over the next decade.

Tipping Point

At some point, parts or all of New Hampshire will reach a tipping point. There will be no workforce growth, healthcare costs for the rapidly growing older population will balloon, more businesses unable to find employees will simply go elsewhere, and economic growth as we know it will cease.

This is a bleak but entirely avoidable future. All that is required is for members and especially leaders of our towns to speak up about the need for a balanced community where people of modest means can live and work, and where young families are welcome. They need to speak out about the myth that allowing workforce housing will increase property taxes. And they need to speak out about the long-term damage inflicted by the injustice of discriminating against young people when housing is age-restricted. We need to take the thumbs off the scale, and stop asking struggling young families to pick up the tab for senior tax discounts.

This is not to suggest or advocate no limits on residential development, or that taxpayers should just accept continued rapid increases in property taxes. But we must stop blaming children, and start looking for the real reasons why we still have sprawl development and rising property taxes, despite modest or no material growth in either children or residents.

Case in Point I

This Is Your Hometown; Too Bad You Can't Live Here

Close intergenerational ties formed between families over many years are the foundation of community life, and of the institutions that contribute to the quality of life enjoyed by all residents. It's only natural, a long-standing cultural tradition, that many young people choose to settle and work and raise their own children in the town that helped nurture them. "I think it's an instinct with the kids," observes Pete Chapman, a 60-year-old small-business owner with deep family roots in the town of Stratham, New Hampshire. "It's tough for kids who were born and raised and grew up here—and then they can't move back into town." Pete's son Jonathan, 27, is one of countless young adults who are unable to rent, buy, or build a home in their own hometown.

Chapmans have lived and worked in Stratham for a long time. The New Hampshire Department of Fish & Game named its all-tide public landing on the Squamscott River "Chapman's Landing" for Pete's uncle. Russell Chapman and his wife had owned the site for decades, and lived in a cottage next to the old bait shack, a local landmark. Pete's uncle Carl Chapman's vegetable stand and small farm were another local landmark, on Portsmouth Avenue where mini-malls reign today.

Asked how long his family has lived in Stratham, Pete replies, "I don't know—a long time. My grandmother was half Indian." Pete still lives in town, where he also runs his business, Stratham Excavators, Inc. He and his wife, Charlan, who goes by Charlie, own 18.5 acres of land where their home and business are located. But Pete says that due to the configuration of the land and its limited road access, local zoning regulations won't allow them to build a second home on the site for their son and his young family.

Jonathan, lean and tanned from working outdoors, says his hometown and its environs is a nice area. He, and others like him, would like to come back to his hometown, he says, "probably just because we grew up there. I went to school in Stratham and Exeter." He has family there, and a job in his family's business. He operates construction equipment and drives a dump truck for his father, often doing site work for new homes far beyond his price range.

"This town has changed," says Pete. "All they want is people with $700,000 homes. They think they're getting ahead with such expensive houses." Pete hopes Jonathan will take over the business in a few years. But they face the same generational transfer problem as many other small-business owners located in pricey real estate markets. He doesn't see how the excavating business will generate enough money for Jonathan to buy from his parents the property where the business is located.

For now and for the foreseeable future, Jonathan and his wife, Megan, are living in a rented trailer in Eliot, Maine. Their first child, a boy they named Mason, was born in June 2007.

Case in Point II

Greener Pastures for All Generations at Nubanusitt Neighborhood and Farm

Shelley and Robin Hulbert are farmers at heart who enjoy the closeness and community of good neighbors. "We were living in a duplex in in-town Peterborough where there was a real sense of neighborhood and people who care about each other," says Shelley, "but we really wanted to farm." So they moved with their children two miles out of town. "We got cows and gardens—and isolation."

When they learned that a 113-acre parcel of land in West Peterborough was on the market, it seemed the perfect spot for an idea that had been hatching in Shelley's mind for some time. "It would be a shame to cut that beautiful farmland and wooded river frontage into a three-acre lot subdivision, or have an individual buy the land and historic Governor Steele house as an estate," she says.

Instead, she and her cohorts have turned it into New Hampshire's first co-housing development, designed around a neighborhood farm. Co-housing is a planned community concept that originated in Denmark. Housing can be more compact because larger common spaces provide for entertaining, preparing and serving community meals, and so on. Cars and parking are kept out of the heart of the community, promoting a healthier environment. "We can have our neighborhood, and have a farm," Shelley says, "a development that connects the greater community to the natural world."

Shelley's friend Sue Chollet, a Smart Growth advocate who chaired Peterborough's master plan steering committee, was one of the first to join the project. Now 63, Sue has been widowed 16 years, managing her 170-acre farm, her horses, and vegetable garden on her own. "There's a restricted-age community at the end of my street. I was on the board of directors. It's not for me," says the former teacher. "I like lots of action—being around kids, and horses."

Nubanusitt Neighborhood and Farm caters to the growing demand for homes close to farms, with opportunities for residents to participate in farming activities. The *Wall Street Journal* recently ran a real estate report headlined "Condo with View of Chicken Coop." Shelley and her collaborators created a plan where residences and farming coexist, fitting right in with strong interest in the region, she says, "in sustainable agriculture, Slow Food, and localvores."

The Monadnock region has one of several New Hampshire Slow Food chapters. The Slow Food movement was started in Italy to celebrate good, well-prepared food and its importance to family and community, as the antithesis of fast food. Localvores are people who prefer and seek out locally and regionally grown and produced foods, for reasons of taste and nutrition, to support local farmers and businesses, and for the environmental benefits from reduced transportation and keeping local and regional land in agriculture.

Shelley and Sue envision what they call "interdependent micro-enterprises" on the land, all managed organically. In addition to the Hulberts' small herd of six to eight dairy cows, there will be horses, chickens for eggs, and perhaps pigs and chickens for meat. They are seeking to attract a vegetable farmer to operate a CSA (Community Supported Agriculture) farm. "We hope to provide as much food as possible for the neighbors," Shelley says. "We hope up to half the community's food will be produced on the property."

"Affordable housing is important, so young farmers can afford to live there," Sue adds. They had planned to build more than the now likely four of the development's 29 single-family homes to sell at prices qualifying for the state's Housing Finance Authority's assistance.

"Our goals are at odds," Shelley laments. "We want our community to be intergenerational, and not exclusive socioeconomically. But we do want quality construction and environmentally sustainable, green buildings—it costs to build what we're building." Although it had not yet been secured in writing, the town had agreed to tax units sold at below-market rates based on actual purchase price, as long as deeds of the affordable units were restricted.

Shelley and Sue see the recent rezoning as a mixed-use district of the West Peterborough area, where the property is located, as an advantage, as their goal is to create a full, vibrant neighborhood where people can work close to where they live. The Governor Steele house has been rehabbed for office and studio space—for residents or others. If community residents want, the fully handicap-accessible Common House could be used to offer educational or commercial activities.

Four houses are ADA-compliant, and all could be easily adapted. Shelley stresses the founders' desire for a diverse community that embraces and supports its members through all stages of life, from birth to death.

CHAPTER 4

🌿 Consequences for Higher Education and Health Care

Children playing baseball in a Deerfield town league

Higher education and health care are major employers in New Hampshire, providing over 82,000 jobs in 2006, or more than one in every seven jobs in the state. These two industries have three important advantages vital to the state's economy: they are stable employers relative to other, more cyclical industries; they provide year-round high-paying professional jobs; and, unlike manufacturing, the jobs are not easily exportable to low-wage countries.

Employment in both industries has been growing over the past several years at a much faster than average pace. Health care services have created more than 1,200 new jobs each year since 2002, increasing at over 2.5% a year.

However, health care and higher education are both increasingly under stress because of statewide demographic shifts not of their making. The vital role they play in the state, and in communities where they are located, means that higher education and health care can also be part of the solution to the exodus of young workers.

Higher Education

Approximately 70,000 students are enrolled full- or part time in New Hampshire's 33 colleges and universities. Even though nearly half those students are from out of state, the institutions depend on a steady supply of college-ready graduates from New Hampshire's 84 high schools. That supply is on track to shrink steadily over the next decade, due to the persistent decline in the number of families with children.

The National Center for Educational Statistics projects that in 10 years, 19% fewer students will be graduating from New Hampshire

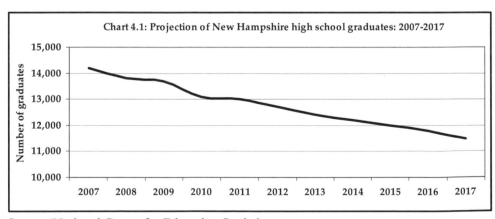

Source: National Center for Education Statistics

The number of new high school graduates in New Hampshire is projected to decline every year for at least the next decade.

high schools. If the present 56% rate of college enrollment for graduating high school seniors holds steady, this would result in a cumulative loss of almost 3,000 first-year college students.

Half of New Hampshire's college-bound high school seniors leave the state for college. That's far above the national average of 18%. But it is also significantly higher than other New England states, where fewer than 40% leave their state. Perhaps one reason is the high cost of tuition and lack of state scholarship funding.

New Hampshire has the highest community college tuition in the nation and the second-highest public four-year tuition. That is not being offset with much financial aid. New Hampshire's average scholarship grant in the 2004–2005 school year was under $700, the lowest by far in New England.

The result is that New Hampshire college graduates leave school with the highest average debt load in the nation: $22,800—nearly twice the national average of $11,700. Coupled with the high price of housing in the state, such a great student loan debt increases the pressure pushing young adults out of the state to places that are more affordable.

The burden of student debt casts an even longer shadow over those who pursue an advanced degree. Carrying student debt for an undergraduate or graduate degree hampers the ability of young adults to purchase a home. Those who start families worry about saving for their own children's education while still saddled with their student debt.

Nearly one in three adults in New Hampshire hold a college degree, eighth highest in the nation. That rate increased significantly over the last 20 years, due to an influx of working-age degree-holders, which has since ceased. This pushed the state's median family income to $67,000 in 2005, fifth highest among all states, and $10,000 above that of Vermont and $15,000 above Maine. Yet Vermont's average scholarship grant in 2004–2005 was $1,500 and Maine's was $860.

One might expect that a state with so many college graduates and such high family income levels would spend more to support the education of future workers. This is particularly so when we consider that it was college graduates who propelled that income upward, and most better-paying jobs will require at least some college education.

This is but another example of a social trap, described in chapter 3. It is clearly in the best interest of New Hampshire as a whole to have more college graduates working in the state, earning higher-than-average wages, and contributing to the state's economic growth. But it is not in the short-term interest of any one taxpayer to fund higher scholarships, or of any one town to provide affordable work-force housing for those recent college graduates.

The consequence is that in New Hampshire, for the first time in its history, residents approaching retirement age are more likely to have a college degree than are young adults. As those older workers retire, employers who need more highly skilled workers will have even greater difficulty finding employees than they do now. Among those employers are the state's institutions of higher education which collectively employ more than 18,000 people, many of them college graduates.

Some college graduates will earn starting salaries as high as $44,000 a year, or about $3,700 a month, which nets after federal taxes to a little under $3,000 a month. This means that even new college graduates considering higher-earning jobs in New Hampshire, where median monthly rental costs exceed $1,000, will most likely be paying one-third or more of their net income for a place to live. That puts New Hampshire employers at a disadvantage when recruiting entry-level workers.

The state of New Hampshire's economy gained a substantial competitive edge when large numbers of college graduates moved here during the 1980s and 1990s, when housing was far less expensive and student debt was minimal.

Unless the out-migration of young adults is reversed, and there is a recovery in the supply of recent college graduates able to live and work in the state over the next decade, the economic advantage the state enjoys from having a more highly skilled workforce will vanish.

Case in Point I

The Chancellor's 55% Campaign: Market New Hampshire to Its College Graduates

Each year 16,000 individuals earn diplomas and certificates from New Hampshire colleges and universities. Every year more than half leave the state. "This departure of more than 8,000 educated individuals represents a huge brain drain and only darkens our future employment picture," says Stephen Reno, chancellor of the University System of New Hampshire (USNH). "As a state, we need to encourage more of these people to stay and work in New Hampshire." Reno says enticing just 10% more graduates to stay would have an enormous impact.

While the students of USNH institutions—University of New Hampshire, Plymouth State University, Keene State College, and Granite State College—were on winter break in January 2007, Chancellor Reno was proposing a campaign to keep more college graduates in the state. Speaking to a group of business leaders, he proposed a tourism-like marketing campaign to sell college students on opportunities in New Hampshire. The bow-tied chancellor was nearly bowled over by the enthusiastic response from that business audience. "I really struck a nerve," he says.

For Reno, the campaign to increase the percentage of college graduates staying in the state from 50 to 55 keeps faith with the charge the USNH Board of Trustees gave him when he was hired in 2000. "I was asked to raise the profile of the University System, and show its critical relationship to the economy of the state," he recalls. On advice of his search committee chair, Trustee and Commissioner of Agriculture, Markets and Food Steve Taylor, Reno began by crisscrossing the state to meet with community and business leaders.

More recently the chancellor, who is a member of Governor Lynch's Jobs Cabinet, tagged along when the governor held a series of seven listening sessions with local business leaders and employers around the state. What he hears over and over from business and community services leaders confirms the trends discussed in this book: Employers are having a difficult time recruiting the people they need.

"We know our state is graying," Reno says. The University System is closely tracking the projected "softening, leveling, slight decline" of high school graduates coming down the pipeline. "In the current workforce, more people are closer to retiring than beginning their careers," he says. UNH Professor of Business Ross Gittell points to the slowing in-migration of educated workers and the pending retirement of the baby boomers."

Businesses will not come—or stay—in New Hampshire if getting an adequate workforce is a big hassle, Reno warns. To stem the flow of educated young people out of the state, he is urging higher education, business, and government to work together in a comprehensive effort to showcase the employment opportunities and quality of life advantages that New Hampshire offers college graduates.

The chancellor conservatively calculates that increasing the number of new graduates who stay and work in New Hampshire by just 10% would add 629 employees to the workforce and have a $42 million impact on the state's economy. If sustained over five years, the cumulative impact would be some 3,100 more employees and an economic benefit exceeding $600 million.

Such a shift could help make New Hampshire a more youthful state and stimulate entrepreneurial ideas and new businesses. It might even have a ripple effect on high school graduates—half of whom currently leave New Hampshire to attend college. New Hampshire colleges and universities do attract many students from out of state, and Reno hopes more of them will also choose to establish careers and start families in New Hampshire communities.

The chancellor's office is working with the University of New Hampshire Survey Center and with public and private colleges in the state to survey college seniors to find out how they make decisions about jobs and locations. Reno has a 55% Initiative Web page and blog devoted to generating ideas and collaboration on this effort (see www. usnh.unh.edu/initiatives/55.shtml).

Don't Go

Facing the same demographic problems as New Hampshire, Vermont's legislature has created the Next Generation Committee to study the issue and recommend steps for marketing a DON'T GO message to graduating college students. Vermont legislators recognize that younger people are vital to Vermont's future tax base, workforce, and schools. The Next Generation Committee has urged adoption of a "green" energy branding effort, reaching out to former Vermonters and forging stronger connections with universities and colleges.

Vermont Governor Jim Douglas has proposed Promise Scholarships as incentives for younger workers to stay in Vermont. Legislators are working on a program of tax credits for employers who hire recent graduates of Vermont colleges or people originally from Vermont. Student surveys show young people appreciate the quality of life in Vermont, and 57% believe they could afford to live in the state. But only 23% see economic opportunities for workers and entrepreneurs there.

Peter Odierna, executive director of the Bennington County Industrial Corp., told the *Rutland Herald* he finds that perceived lack of opportunity "absolutely maddening." Odierna said industrial employers in Bennington County can not fill the available jobs. The number of industrial jobs in Bennington County went up 6% in 2006, according to Odierna. He's concerned about availability of affordable housing, too—especially rentals sought by younger workers.

The New England Board of Higher Education (NEBHE) is addressing the out-migration of young people from the entire region. It has proposed a regional campaign, called College Ready New England, to target high school seniors. The hope for this campaign, still in the formation stage, is that all six New England states will develop individual efforts to encourage students to stay in their home state for higher education.

The New Hampshire College & University Council, with funding from the New Hampshire Higher Education Assistance Foundation and in cooperation with the New Hampshire High

Technology Council, has launched a Web site to link New Hampshire businesses with New Hampshire college students seeking internships and/or entry-level positions. This site, www.intern2careernh.com, is an important and free service for employers, and for students and graduates seeking to stay and work in New Hampshire.

These marketing efforts to encourage New Hampshire's young people to pursue higher education and first career opportunities in their home state are critical to addressing the disturbing demographic trends confronting the state. But these efforts alone cannot stem the tide of out-migration of our youth from New Hampshire.

A critical element to reversing that tide involves tackling the high tuition costs for students and families that results from low state funding for higher education. Higher education leaders also point to the critical need for housing options that are affordable for young professionals and workers.

Healthcare Providers

There are more than 2,000 medical offices and nearly 300 nursing homes or other residential care facilities in New Hampshire that are served by, or associated with, 27 general hospitals and six specialty hospitals. As the state's third largest employment sector, after retail and manufacturing, healthcare providers employ some 64,000 workers.

Nearly all New Hampshire hospitals are not-for-profit organizations, and they provide substantial community benefit. For example, they offer charity care and support community health centers and an array of other services.

The extraordinary growth of older people in New Hampshire—a 23% increase in the age-55-or-older residents since 2000 versus a 2% increase in under-age-55 residents—means demand for healthcare and medical service workers will continue to rise for the foreseeable future. The addition since 2000 of more than 3,500 units of housing restricted to residents ages 55 or older, almost all in the southern part of the state, has only accelerated this growth.

Despite the increasing demand for services, hospitals and other healthcare providers cannot find enough of the workers that they need now. Exeter Health Resources, for example, which usually has about 2,200 employees, had over 140 unfilled positions during the first half of 2007. One of the reasons given by prospective employees for turning down job offers is their inability to find affordable housing.

Forecasts by the New Hampshire Economic and Labor Market Information Bureau suggest that this problem will get worse. They project that healthcare providers in the state will need at least 21,000 new workers over the next 10 years, a 34% increase over today. That's the highest rate of increase of any industry—and it does not include new hires needed to cover normal employee attrition.

The conventional answer to a need for so many new workers in a tight labor market is to increase wages and salaries. Most corporations that could raise prices would certainly consider that strategy. But almost no medical services or healthcare providers have much control over what they are paid for their care. Those payments are set by insurance companies through negotiation with the healthcare providers or by the Centers for Medicare & Medicaid Services. For some time now, the payments by Medicare and Medicaid—which are not negotiable—have not covered the cost of the care provided.

In 2005, Medicaid's underpayment to New Hampshire hospitals hit a record high of $63 million, almost double the 2001 underpayment of $32 million. Medicare underpayment that year was also a record $157 million, a 153% increase from 2001. The consequence: a rapid increase in what is known as cost shifting—whereby hospitals charge patients insured by private insurance companies ever-larger amounts to make up for the below-cost care they must provide. As a result, employers in the state are either paying higher health insurance premiums for their workers or passing those higher costs onto those employees.

During 2005, Medicare and Medicaid payments were nearly half (47%) of New Hampshire hospitals' gross patient revenue. After cost shifting to private payers, that percentage was reduced to 35% of net patient revenue, according to the New Hampshire Center for Public Policy Studies. This cost shifting has been a big factor in the rising cost of health insurance for employers and individuals. In some cases, it has resulted in individuals joining the ranks of those with little or no health insurance.

But projections by Tom Duffy, at the state's Office of Energy & Planning, suggest that the fraction of revenues hospitals receive from Medicare and Medicaid will only get a lot bigger and the fraction received from private insurers may actually shrink.

Duffy projects that from 2005 to 2015, the number of New Hampshire residents age 55 or older will increase 50%, resulting in 80,000 additional Medicare- or Medicaid-covered individuals. During that same period, however, he projects the number of working-age residents ages 20 to 55 will decline 5%, resulting in a loss of about 35,000 residents, most of whom would normally be working and covered by some form of private health insurance.

These stark demographic trends suggest that at some point soon, the clear majority of payments to hospitals will be from Medicaid or Medicare. As that fraction of below-cost payers grows, it will become financially impossible for private insurance firms to absorb the shifted costs—those costs will simply be too large to pass along to employers or to be borne by individuals.

This scenario can be avoided. If not, it could be an economic disaster. If communities across the state continue to provide ever-larger tax abatements to senior citizens and permit only age-restricted or very expensive housing in order to exclude young families with children, then the consequences for the state's healthcare providers are grave indeed.

On the other hand, if communities begin to see the impact of heavily favoring one age group and excluding another and if they change course, then the future will play out differently. If New Hampshire communities begin to work together to find ways to permit more truly affordable workforce housing, it will be much easier for all employers, including those in health care, to find workers.

If New Hampshire's employers could just fill the thousands of job vacancies they have now, it would add significantly to the rolls of the privately insured, and help to offset the rapid growth of those on Medicaid or Medicare.

The state's healthcare system is in need of some preventive medicine, which requires a major shift in voter attitudes in New Hampshire cities and towns. First, other people's children must no longer be viewed as an intolerable financial burden. Children should be recognized instead as a vital component in securing our communities' future.

Second, provision of affordable workforce housing must be understood as an essential contribution to the overall well-being of all communities in the state.

Third, local planning and development decisions deserve greater awareness of how what we do as citizens and voters has substantial consequences beyond our town or city borders. Childproof housing and exclusionary five-acre lot zoning will ultimately harm us all.

Case in Point II

Hospital's Answer to Workforce Housing Needs: Build It

"The high cost of housing affects our employment at the hospital," says Peter Gosline, president and CEO of Monadnock Community Hospital in Peterborough. Hiring nurses is a challenge, and people working in the hospital's support departments are commuting longer and longer distances. Historically, he observes, the hospital had owned at least one house in town for nurses in need of a place to stay.

The hospital recently received approval for construction of a road that will connect Route 202 with the current hospital access. The new road will cross a large parcel of hospital-owned land, opening it up for planned development. The town had already approved this hospital land as one of three new mixed-use districts, which can accommodate more affordable types of housing.

The Monadnock Economic Development Corporation helped the hospital obtain Community Development Block Grant funds to help build the connector road. Plans for developing the hospital land begin with a medical office building, and then a clinical service building to house emergency, radiology, surgical, and other medical services.

These first phases of development will position the hospital financially for the housing component in four to seven years. Gosline wants to provide both workforce housing and aging-in-place housing. He sees "a certain chemistry" in pairing these two, but, he says, "we need to do a feasibility study. Our goal is to enable people to stay in their homes as long as possible. People become depressed when they have to move," he says.

"The town is conservative—we can't do anything overnight," Gosline says. "We've got to involve people in the process. We will work with the town and our neighbors through an open process. Everything we do is a test of credibility for the next thing we do." The hospital's new wellness center is an example, he says. "Some neighbors were critical—but now they love it."

The Monadnock region has become a destination, Gosline says, leaving local workers at a disadvantage in the housing game. "If your job pays less than $70,000 a year, you can't afford to live here."

CHAPTER 5

🌿 Bitter Fruits: Workforce, Public Education, and Political Consequences

A Marlborough resident (Maidli Hill) speaking at one of the meetings to decide about building a new school

W orkforce growth is the cornerstone of economic growth. Periods of recession are defined by the absence of workforce growth. So we should view with alarm the growing worker shortages in New Hampshire, and the forecasts for even slower workforce growth in the future.

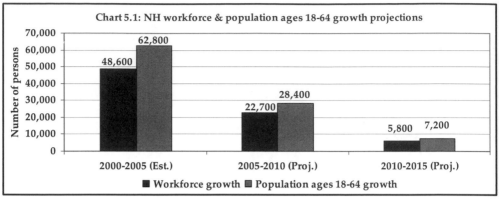

Source: NH Economic and Labor Market Information Bureau

Workforce growth is projected to shrink to nearly zero within the next 10-15 years.

Workforce Impact

In chapter 4, we reported on the great difficulty Exeter Health Resources is having filling more than 140 vacant positions. It can't compete with employers in other parts of the country, where the same wage goes farther because of lower housing costs.

Prospective employees for a healthcare provider in southern New Hampshire, looking for places to live within a 20 to 25 minute commute, find that a great many of the homes built in the last six years that would be affordable to the average healthcare worker are open only to applicants age 55 or older.

If the typical after-tax pay for those open Exeter Health Resources jobs is $50,000, which is about the average wage for Rockingham County healthcare workers, then the Exeter area is losing out on 140 times $50,000, or $7 million, annually in consumer economic activity for as long as those jobs go unfilled.

This can have a significant impact on retailers, restaurants, and other businesses. These businesses in turn may hire fewer people, because business is slower than it might otherwise be. Multiply this relatively small Exeter area situation over communities across the state, and the economic impact of not being able to attract even above-average-wage workers is quite substantial.

Where Have All the Workers Gone?

Chart 5.1 shows the estimated growth of the New Hampshire workforce between 2000 and 2005, and then projects that growth over the next ten years based on the state's Office of Energy & Planning's projected increases in the working-age population.

Over the first five years of this decade, New Hampshire's working-age population increased by an estimated 62,800 people. According to the Bureau of Labor Statistics, about 77% of them were in the paid labor force. For purposes of projecting workforce growth, we assumed that in future years, with more open positions, that fraction will increase to 80% percent.

Even so, labor force growth over the next decade is projected to slow to a trickle, in large part because so much of the working-age population left the state in the previous decade. The heart of the experienced and productive workforce—people ages 35 to 54—is expected to drop by 65,000 from 2005 to 2015, which could mean a loss of more than 50,000 potential workers.

Some suggest that we can fill some of the looming worker shortages from the rapidly growing ranks of those ages 65 or older, who in the past were nearly all retired. For some jobs, and some individuals, that might be possible. But even in the most optimistic projection by the Bureau of Labor Statistics, only 20% to 25% of people age 65 or older will be available to work, full or part-time. The age 65 or older population in New Hampshire is projected to increase by 83,000 people by 2015. Even if the full 25% were available to work full time (a highly unlikely event), that would gain back only about 20,000 workers—hardly enough to make up for losses in younger people.

Can We Make Them Feel Wanted?

The brightest hope for the future is in the projected 16% growth in the 25-to-34 year-old age cohort—a gain of 24,000 people—by 2015. But they will stay in New Hampshire only if they find places to live that are reasonably affordable based on their income. The extent

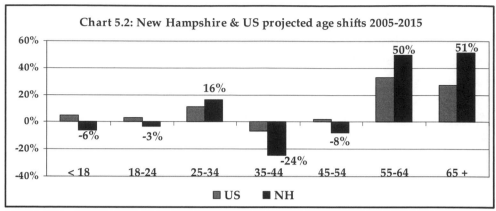

Source: Census Bureau and NH Department of Energy & Planning population projections

New Hampshire is projected to gain older residents and lose children and working age adults at a significantly faster rate than the nation.

of our state's future economic prosperity will depend heavily on the willingness of towns and cities to permit a sufficient amount of workforce housing—starter homes for those who can purchase and rental units for those who are not ready for homeownership. Only then will young adults who want to stay in New Hampshire take one of the many jobs that are now open.

Impact on School-related Voting Patterns

The decline of young adults in the past, and the present shrinking number of children, has made families with school-age kids a decreasing minority of households in most New Hampshire towns and school districts. Back in 1990, almost one in three households (30%) in the state were married couples with children under age 18. At that time, they were equal in number to married couples with no children at home. But by 2006, the married-with-children-under-18 share of households had shrunk to 22%—below one in four. Today there are 125 empty-nester married-couple households in New Hampshire for every 100 married couples with kids.

One example is the small town of Newmarket, in Rockingham County. Back in 1990, some 26% of households were married couples. But by 2000 that figure had slipped to less than 22%, and it is estimated to be under 20% today. Finding a suitable site in the town added to the challenges, but twice in the past two years voters have rejected by an overwhelming majority proposals to build a new middle/high school.

Part of the issue around financing public education in Newmarket, and many other New Hampshire communities, is the exceedingly small size of the school districts. Newmarket has only about 1,100 students (the same number as a decade ago) in a town with just 9,200 residents and about 4,000 households.

In an August 2006 warning to the people of New Hampshire, Mike Pride, editor-in-chief of *The Concord Monitor,* told of the demographic changes that overwhelmed his own hometown of Clearwater, Florida, 30 years ago. "Clearwater always had booming growth," but since his own boyhood the growth was as "a haven for retirees," Pride wrote "School bonds failed because so many voters had no children in the schools." The deterioration of education drove Pride to move his young family out of the area. The job at the *Monitor* and the city's schools lured him to Concord. Now he sees his adopted state becoming "a mecca for people 55 and over," and a telltale pattern "even in progressive communities" of weakening support for public education, he says.

Voters—an increasing fraction of them retired—are understandably reluctant to vote for larger school budgets and expensive new school buildings when the number of students is shrinking. The tendency, however, has been to ascribe rising costs to the perception of rapidly increasing numbers of students. This gives voice to the popular public policy notion that permitting only childproof housing, or better yet no housing, will prevent school-related expenses, and thus property taxes, from rising.

Unfortunately, the reality is that school budgets, which are mostly fixed costs and contractual obligations, do not get smaller when the number of children declines. In a vicious cycle these actions are compounding the problem. Among the reasons that school budgets do not get smaller are the rising cost of health insurance for school district employees (see chapter 4 on cost-shifting) and the higher salaries that must be paid so that teachers and administrators can afford housing within a reasonable commute from their schools.

But when the number of children declines over a period of time, so too does the number of parents of children. Those parents are a significant part of the workforce, as well as among the largest contributors to local retail sales. That shrinkage has serious economic implications.

Political Implications

New Hampshire has two congressional representatives. But of even greater importance on the national scene has been its hold on the first-in-the-nation presidential primary. Many other states are fighting hard to wrest away that long-held status, and the reason they give is simple. They say New Hampshire has aged so much in the past 20 years, and has so few minorities, that it can no longer fairly represent the nation.

Those other states may not succeed in 2008. But the days of holding the nation's first primary are numbered without an influx of young people, similar to what the state experienced in the 1980s. Such an influx is the best hope of both rejuvenating the state's population and adding some diversity.

In chapter 1 we explained that the state's population growth has slowed to a crawl, significantly below the national average. Congressional seats are reapportioned after each decennial census, with the next one in 2010. Because populations are growing much more rapidly in other regions, New Hampshire, like other states growing much more slowly than the national average, is in danger of losing one of its two congressional representatives. Maybe not in 2010, but if the state's own slowing growth projections come to pass, it is likely to happen in 2020.

Jared Diamond's recent book, *Collapse,* documents in great detail how societies that cling to cultural beliefs and are organizationally